The Death of Cupcake
A Child's Experience with Loss

Written by
Susan Nicholas, MD

Illustrated by
Basia Tran

Conscious Children's Book Series: Book 2
Illustrated by Basia Tran
Cover Art & Design by Basia Tran
Published by Human Consciousness Consortium Publishing
Atlanta, GA
Paperback ISBN: 978-1-7324336-7-0
Hardcover ISBN: 978-1-7324336-5-6
E-book ISBN: 978-1-7324336-6-3
Library of Congress Control Number: 2020908264

To the children of the world who have lost a loved one.
Special thanks to Wolfie, Jack, and Savvy...
And in loving memory of Cupcake, Grandma & Grandpa.

S.N.

For everything, there is a season.

Just as the seasons change in a cycle of renewal,

Our human lives also follow a cycle.

At the end of life, the body becomes like the fallen leaves. But we do not have to be sad about a dying body because we are much more than a physical body. We are without end.

When someone dies, it is
like the metamorphosis of
a caterpillar, moving from
one state of being into
another. The caterpillar
does not die, it transforms.

We do not mourn the caterpillar
that becomes a butterfly.
Instead we marvel at the beauty
of the transformation.

And just like when a caterpillar becomes a butterfly, our beloved pets shed their bodies when they die, and move onto another enriching experience.

The body is temporary, but the soul is infinite.
It goes on forever.

15

It is natural to feel sad when you have a memory about your pet who has died. Your beloved will be deeply missed. But remember, your pet is okay now and not in any pain.

"Daddy, Grandma has learned enough, so it was time for her to leave."

18

Our loved ones shed their bodies too and move
onto a more enriching experience.

When we die, our bodies that remain are like empty shells. Remember, though we may miss our loved ones, there is nothing sad about an empty shell.

"It was a shock, but I know Grandma is fine."

24

Grandpa is looking down on me and protecting me. I can feel it.
I'm so shocked that Grandpa has died. I feel really sad.
Me too.

The body is born on Earth and remains on Earth. But after we die, we continue on as pure energy. Our energy body is where our consciousness lives. Consciousness animates our bodies during our lifetime on Earth.

When we leave our bodies on Earth, we can exist in a different kind of body that is as light as a feather...or as pure conscious energy in a point of light.

We all feel grief
in our own way and
grieving takes time.

Though you may feel sad when you think about a pet or a loved one who has died, eventually you will be celebrating the change of season and the cycle of life once again.

31

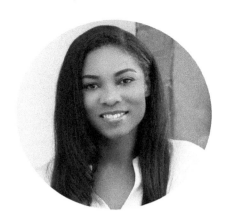

About the Author

Susan Nicholas, MD, is an author, international speaker, serial entrepreneur, healer, and host of the Be Conscious Podcast for SusanNicholas.org. Her diverse works speak of the universal message to awaken humanity to consciousness.

Dr. Nicholas is the founder of the Human Consciousness Consortium Publishing and the author of **The Duality of Being: Perspectives from Multidimensional Travel** and **Two Parts of Me: I Am More Than My Body. The Death of Cupcake** is the second title in the series of **Conscious Children's Books** exposing the intersection of grief and consciousness. It is designed to guide parents and children through their deepest feelings about death from a conscious perspective. The book highlights the true feelings of children who have experienced the loss of a pet or loved one. Children have lent their likenesses and stories, sharing their most intimate thoughts and feelings.

Susan is a thought leader on human consciousness and is often found contemplating the interplay of essence and form. She is a French language and culture enthusiast, and in her free time can be found organic baking, swimming, and exploring magnificence in nature.

She and her son are currently based in Atlanta, GA.

About the Illustrator

Basia Tran is a Polish-Vietnamese children's books illustrator based in Jersey City, NJ, where she lives with her husband, Evan. Her diverse work and interests are all connected by a common thread: her desire to tell stories that could make you laugh or teach you something new and fun :)

In her free time, Basia is rock climbing, enjoying jasmine green tea or dog-sitting with her husband.

You can find her on:
Instagram - www.instagram.com/basiatran
Facebook - www.facebook.com/basiatranart
Website - www.basiatran.com

Author's Note

The Death of Cupcake: A Child's Experience With Loss is my second title in a series of **Conscious Children's Books** published by the Human Consciousness Consortium. The aim is to create an illustrated children's series that addresses the conversations we have the most difficulty having with our children. This title came to me after the release of my first children's book: **Two Parts of Me: I Am More Than My Body.** From my energy healing practice and through the lens of consciousness, I came to realize that many children are not given the space to make closure when a loved one transitions because physical death is not readily discussed. Furthermore, many children are excluded from funeral or burial proceedings. Thereby, the unresolved feelings and emotions surrounding the death of a close family member or friend are often carried into adulthood.

I wondered if by involving children in the conversations surrounding death, might we learn from them, and in doing so create a space for them to grieve to completion. If we, as a global community could perceive death as a transformation, would we not overcome our false fears of finality, recognizing the refined eloquence of passing.

The Death of Cupcake was written to remind parents and children of their infinite nature. Death is a liberation, and for many the final unconscious moment of their human existence.

Future **Conscious Children's Book** titles include the topics of gender identity, bullying, learning and physical differences. Future titles will also introduce children to the energy of money to break cycles of generational poverty and the resulting diminished self-worth. All children's titles are non-fiction and written from a child's perspective with conscious awareness infused throughout the pages. Titles in this series are designed for children in kindergarten through 4th grade and ages 5-10 years.

"Dr. Susan Nicholas'... beautiful explanation of the energy body has created a powerful companion to any conversation about death, loss and grief. The illustrations by Basia Tran are rich and moving."

-**Tricia Brouk**, International Award Winning Director, Producer and The Founder of The Big Talk.

"A must-have for every child's bookshelf. An enlightened perspective on a tough (but inevitable) subject, simply and beautifully presented."

-**Todd Johnson, Esq.**

"This pioneering book of enlightenment helps kids understand that while a loved one is gone from their sight, our loved one's spirit lives on. I highly recommend this amazing book."

-**Lisa Hartman, DNP**

Follow the Human Consciousness Consortium on Facebook or visit us at www.SusanNicholas.org

Susan Nicholas, MD
BE CONSCIOUS

35

CPSIA information can be obtained
at www.ICGtesting.com
Printed in the USA
LVHW072059181122
733026LV00037B/57